GW00691822

Arnica

Also known as:

Leopard's Bane.

Uses:

Arthritic and rheumatic pain, fibromyalgia, sports injuries and other inflammatory pain.

Description:

Arnica is a perennial herb with a bright yellow flower that blooms in July. It has been used in homoeopathic medicine for hundreds of years but has now been discovered to possess powerful anti-inflammatory action when used externally as a herbal preparation.

How it works:

Arnica contains active components that have a marked anti-inflammatory action. A pain-killing and anti-oedematous effect results from this action.

Arnica also stimulates the activity of white blood cells that disperse congested blood, and releases fluid from bruised or traumatised areas, stimulating circulation and acting against bacterial infection. It inhibits the action of an enzyme that destroys inflamed tissue, thus having a tissue-protective action.

Additional advice:

For external use only. Avoid in known allergy to Arnica or the Asteraceae (daisy) family.

Artichoke

Also known as:

Globe Artichoke, Cynara scolymus.

Uses:

Reduces cholesterol levels, stimulates liver function, protects the liver, helps metabolise fats, gallstones.

Description:

Artichokes grow easily in the warmer Mediterranean climate. It is often found as part of the diet of those living in these countries and considered to be a luxury food. Like Milk Thistle, the plant belongs to the daisy family. It grows to a height of about two metres, producing large violet flowers.

Artichokes have a bitter taste due to the presence of cynaropicrin, which is found only in the green parts of the plant.

How it works:

Apart from cynaropicrin which stimulates liver function through its 'bitterness', artichokes contain another valuable substance known as cynarin. This has very specific properties, protecting and enhancing liver function in a way similar to silymarin which is found in Milk Thistle.

Artichokes also contain a group of compounds known as phenolic acids which have the ability to reduce blood cholesterol and lipid levels through an action on the liver.

Additional advice:

Medical opinion should be sought when acute or chronic liver conditions are present.

THREAD VEINS

Aesculus (Horse Chestnut)
Strengthens veins.

Vinca minor
Improves blood vessel tone throughout the body.

THRUSH

Echinacea
Antifungal and immune-boosting.

Spilanthes
Antifungal — take internally and dilute to use as a douche.

TINNITUS

Ginkgo biloba
Improves blood supply to the head.

Plantago
Reduces catarrhal congestion in the ear/nose/throat tract.

Valerian
May help if condition is stress-related.

Vinca minor
Increases tone of blood vessels.

TONSILITIS

Echinacea
Antibacterial and antiviral.

Calendula
Anti-inflammatory and cleansing herb.

Salvia (Sage)
Gargle with diluted tincture.

TRAVEL SICKNESS

Ginger
Suitable for all ages.

URINARY TRACT INFECTIONS

Uva-ursi
Anti-infective for the urinary tract.

Echinacea
Boosts immunity and clears infection.

URTICARIA

See PRICKLY HEAT

Hypericum (St John's Wort)
Deals with nerve pain. Take the tincture internally and apply the oil externally. Also antiviral.

SINUSITIS

Plantago
Clears catarrh from the ear/nose/throat tract.

Echinacea
Anti-infective.

SKIN — dry, itchy, oily

Viola tricolor
Nourishing for all skin conditions.

Neem
Has anti-inflammatory properties. For external use only.

SLEEP DISTURBANCES
See INSOMNIA

SLIMMING
See OVERWEIGHT

SNORING

Marum verum
Restorative for the tissues of the nasal passage.

SORE THROAT

Salvia (Sage)
Gargle with diluted tincture.

Echinacea
Antibacterial and anti-inflammatory.

STRESS

Valerian
Suitable for long term use.

Avena sativa
Gentle and suitable for long term use.

Eleutherococcus (Siberian Ginseng)
Helps the body adapt to physical and emotional stress.

TENDONITIS

Devil's Claw
Anti-inflammatory. Use long term.

Section One
Commonly Used Herbs

Aesculus

Also known as:

Aesculus hippocastanum semen, Horse Chestnut seed.

Uses:

Varicose veins, thread veins, haemorrhoids.

Description:

The use of Aesculus in venous disorders has been recognised for a long time and it has been used as a treatment for various venous conditions since the 19th Century.

It is the seed of the Horse Chestnut tree, instantly recognisable to many children as the 'conker', that is used medicinally. A commonly held belief in the 18th Century was that carrying Horse Chestnut seeds in one's pocket would prevent gout, rheumatism and back pain. There does not seem to be much evidence to support this in modern research.

How it works:

The constituent of Aesculus which has been most studied is aescin. It has the ability to improve the tone of veins, reducing leakage into the surrounding tissue.

Often varicose veins are more troublesome in the summer and starting a course of Aesculus during the early summer can prevent the distressing symptoms during the warmer weather. For best results, I find that a three to four month course is advisable. Those suffering from varicose veins will also benefit from ensuring that constipation is not a factor.

Additional advice:

Best taken with food. Do not use if taking anticoagulants such as Aspirin or Warfarin. Seek advice if pregnant or breastfeeding.

Agnus castus

Also known as:

Chaste Tree, Vitex agnus castus.

Uses:

Premenstrual Syndrome (PMS), teenage acne, period pain, fibroids.

Description:

This herb has a long tradition of use as a general balancer for the female hormones. Despite its common name, Chaste Tree, Agnus castus is actually a shrub found in the Mediterranean. The fruit of the plant is used in phytotherapy and gives off a pleasant peppermint-like smell.

How it works:

Agnus castus acts on the pituitary gland to increase the secretion of luteinising hormone, which leads to an increase in the production of progesterone during the second half of the menstrual cycle. It has also been reported to possess the ability to inhibit prolactin.

Both these actions are thought to be important in PMS, particularly as many who suffer with the problem have a greater sensitivity to prolactin. Agnus castus has also been found to be beneficial in the treatment of acne in both men and women.

Additional advice:

Seek advice from a Healthcare Professional if using oral contraceptives or HRT. Do not use if pregnant or breastfeeding.

Aloe vera

Also known as:

Aloe barbadensis.

Uses:

Healing of wounds and burns, psoriasis.

Description:

Aloe vera has been used in wound healing for thousands of years. The Egyptians used it in 1,500 BC for skin problems and infections. The Greek physician Dioscorides recommended it externally for wounds, haemorrhoids, ulcers and hair loss.

The plant has thick fleshy leaves that contain a clear gel and is easy to grow indoors.

How it works:

The plant contains anthraquinone glycosides, resins and polysacharrides.

When taken internally, Aloe vera has a cleansing effect on the body, by virtue of its action on the digestive tract. This makes it useful for a number of skin conditions, especially psoriasis, where the process of internal detoxification is deemed by naturopaths to be important.

Scientific use of Aloe in wound healing was first documented in 1935. Since then, there have been a number of studies showing its effectiveness as a treatment for burns and other wounds.

Additional advice:

Aloe vera can have a laxative effect. Do not use if pregnant or breastfeeding.

Avena sativa

Also known as:

Oats.

Uses:

Tonic for the nerves, anxiety, nervous exhaustion, ongoing stress, hyperactivity, impotence.

Description:

Oats have been used traditionally as a nerve tonic for hundreds of years. It is the seed which is used medicinally and also for food.

How it works:

Fresh oat seed contains high levels of vitamin B, minerals and other nutrients. These are recognised to be important and beneficial for the proper functioning of the nervous system. Oats contain a group of substances which have a calming effect on the nervous system, the most active of which, gramine, has been shown to relax muscles. The balance of constituents present in oat seed probably accounts for the restorative benefits in depression, states of debility and exhaustion — and the traditional use as a nerve tonic.

Some researchers have found that oats can be beneficial for those who are trying to overcome the symptoms of withdrawal from alcohol and drugs.

Additional advice:

No restrictions on use are known.

Berberis

Also known as:

Barberry, Berberis vulgaris.

Uses:

Gallstones, anti-inflammatory.

Description:

Berberis vulgaris is a perennial shrub, native to Europe. The leaves and berries are used medicinally.

How it works:

Berberis contains the alkaloid berberine, the most well studied of the constituents. It is a powerful antibacterial, effective against disease-bearing microorganisms such as salmonella and E. Coli, making it effective in treating the majority of gastrointestinal infections.

In addition to this, berberine stimulates the secretion of bile and bilirubin, supporting its use for gallstones, obstructive jaundice and sluggish digestive problems.

Additional advice:

Do not take if pregnant or breastfeeding. Consult a Doctor if taking medication for gallstones, liver problems, kidney disease or inflammatory diseases of the gastrointestinal tract. It should not be used in high doses in cases of low blood pressure.

Bilberry

Also known as:

Vaccinium myrtillus, European blueberry.

Uses:

Eye strain, improves vision.

Description:

Bilberry is a shrub which grows in woods and forests throughout Europe. The fruit is blue-black or purple and has a high nutritive value. It has been used for many years as a general tonic for the eyes. It is said that RAF pilots were encouraged to eat bilberries to improve night vision.

How it works:

The main constituents of Bilberries are known as anthocyanosides — a group of flavonoids.

These have the ability to bind to the part of the retina which is responsible for vision, which in turn increases the rate of regeneration of the visual pigments in the retina.

In addition, the substances present in Bilberry have the ability to prevent the destruction of collagen, which is responsible for stabilising the delicate tissue structure of the eyes.

One particular anthocyanidin, myrtillin, has been shown to reduce blood sugar levels.

Additional advice:

No restrictions on use are known.

Black Cohosh

Also known as:

Cimicifuga racemosa.

Uses:

Menopausal symptoms, e.g. hot flushes, aches and pains, low libido.

Description:

This is a member of the Buttercup family, originally used by the Native American Indians for its effect on normalising the female hormones. In modern Phytotherapy, Black Cohosh is used for problems associated with the menopause.

How it works:

The mode of action of Black Cohosh in the treatment of menopausal difficulties is not clear. It seems to act both directly on the tissues of the reproductive system and indirectly through the nervous system.

Black Cohosh contains several important constituents. One group of constituents acts to reduce the concentration of luteinising hormone which, in turn, decreases the relative balance of progesterone in favour of the oestrogens. At the same time, another group has been found to act directly on oestrogen receptors.

It provides a natural source of salicylic acid. This may account for some of the beneficial effects seen with painful menstruation during menopause.

Additional advice:

Do not use if allergic to Aspirin. Consult a Healthcare Professional before use if you are taking oral contraceptives, HRT or Tamoxifen. Do not use if pregnant, breastfeeding or suffering from breast cancer.

Calendula

Also known as:

Marigold, Calendula officinalis.

Uses:

Acne, tonsillitis.

Description:

Marigold is a common garden plant with a long tradition in European Phytotherapy as a treatment for a variety of skin conditions.

How it works:

The active constituents in Calendula officinalis have still to be identified although phytochemical studies have reported flavonoids, volatile oil, carotenoids and triterpenes. The triterpenes appear to be the main active group. The flavonoids may contribute to the anti-inflammatory effect.

Additional advice:

Do not use if pregnant or breastfeeding.

Centaurium

Also known as:

Centaurium umbellatum, Centaury.

Uses:

Acid stomach, indigestion, hiatus hernia, anorexia, appetite loss, heartburn (reflux), food intolerances.

Description:

Centaurium has been used as the classic stomach bitter for many years. Bitter herbs or bitter tasting foods used to form a significant part of the diet. Nowadays, these have practically disappeared with the trend towards more convenient, inoffensive and easy to eat foods.

How it works:

As you may have surmised, Centaurium has a bitter taste and owes this property to the group of compounds called bitter glycosides.

The bitterness of food on the tongue plays a very important role in the digestive process. The taste of bitter foods stimulates the appetite and triggers the secretion of digestive juices in the stomach, which in turn improves the breakdown of food.

At the same time, the hormone gastrin is secreted by the walls of the stomach. This improves the digestive process, by improving the passage of food from the stomach to the intestines. Another important action of gastrin is to tighten the 'valve' between the oesophagus and stomach, which is important in reducing the symptoms associated with a hiatus hernia, such as gastric reflux.

Additional advice:

No restrictions on use are known.

Crataegus

Also known as:

Crataegus oxyacantha, Hawthorn.

Uses:

Heart tonic, high or low blood pressure.

Description:

Hawthorn is a small spiny tree or shrub which is native to Europe. It is often seen growing in hedges.

Hawthorn berries have been used by Phytotherapists as a heart tonic for many years.

How it works:

Crataegus is perhaps one of the most widely used herbs for the heart. The precise mode of action is still unclear — although we do know that the plant does not contain digitalis-like compounds.

Flavonoids found in Crataegus have been found to improve the circulation of the heart and, to a lesser extent, the circulation of other parts of the body. Glycosides present are believed to increase the tone of the heart, improving the force of contraction whilst reducing the rate of contraction — in short, making the heart work more efficiently.

Additional advice:

Inform a Healthcare Professional if you are using Crataegus in addition to any other prescribed medication for the heart.

Dandelion

Also known as:

Taraxacum.

Uses:

Diuretic, water retention, liver and gallbladder tonic, gallstones.

Description:

The Dandelion plant is often seen as a weed. However, it has distinct medicinal properties and its action on the liver and gallbladder has been particularly prized by herbalists.

How it works:

Dandelion is an excellent cleansing agent, being one of the most effective detoxifying herbs. It possesses a wide range of active constituents and is also rich in minerals and nutrients. The plant stimulates liver and particularly gallbladder function.

This has a primary use in improving digestion as a result of an increase in digestive juices. In addition, Dandelion has diuretic and mild laxative properties.

Additional advice:

Those taking diuretics or with liver complaints, gallstones or an obstructed bile duct should firstly consult a Healthcare Professional.

Devil's Claw

Also known as:

Harpagophytum.

Uses:

Anti-inflammatory, arthritis, rheumatism, autoimmune disorders, allergies, sports injuries, fibromyalgia, tendonitis.

Description:

This plant is native to the Southern parts of Africa. It is the tubers (or the storage roots) of the plant, measuring approximately 20cm in length, which are used medicinally.

Devil's Claw is a traditional remedy for general joint pains.

How it works:

Devil's Claw contains a group of components known as iridoids which possess anti-inflammatory, anti-rheumatic and pain killing properties. The anti-inflammatory action has been shown to be equivalent to that of steroids, but the plant itself does not seem to contain this group of compounds.

Recent research has shown that the plant has an action in balancing the immune system, reducing the tendency for allergies and autoimmunity (where the body's immune system attacks normal healthy body cells).

Additional advice:

No restrictions on use are known.

Echinacea

Also known as:
Echinacea purpurea, Purple Coneflower.

Uses:
Immune stimulant, colds, flu, healing of wounds and other minor infections, acne.

Description:
The Echinacea herb is one of the most popular herbs used in Europe. It is considered to be the prime remedy for the immune system and this view has been supported by extensive research. The Native Americans were the first to recognise the value of the plant, using it for wound healing and snakebites.

How it works:
Echinacea works principally by stimulating a group of cells in the immune system known as the macrophages. These cells have the unique ability to 'eat' matter foreign to the body, such as viruses, bacteria and other particulate matter such as dust particles entering the body as a result of air pollution.

Stimulating the immune system in this way improves the way the body handles infections, when viruses and bacteria do manage to invade the body. Whilst there are two other species of Echinacea which may be found in use, tests have shown that Echinacea purpurea has the greatest activity.

Clinical trials have shown that Echinacea can improve the symptoms of colds and flu, shortening the course of the illness in 78% of people.

Additional advice:
If you are currently taking immunosuppressant medication consult a Doctor before using Echinacea.

Eleutherococcus

Also known as:

Eleutherococcus senticosus, Siberian Ginseng.

Uses:

General tonic, stress, fatigue, Chronic Fatigue Syndrome, convalescence, menopause.

Description:

The root of the herb commonly referred to simply as Eleutherococcus, is an example of an 'adaptogen'. This has been defined as a substance which enables the body's metabolism to adapt and cope with unfavourable conditions, such as physical and psychological stress, infections and environmental pollutants.

Eleutherococcus is native to Eastern Asia and particularly Siberia. It bears many similar actions to the more familiar Panax Ginseng.

How it works:

A group of compounds isolated from Eleutherococcus called the 'eleutherosides', which include naturally-occurring steroids, are thought to represent the main active constituents. These have a wide range of activities, which support the body's many processes, giving a revitalising effect. In addition, polysaccharides present have been found to possess the ability to stimulate the immune system.

Additional advice:

Not to be taken by diabetics, epileptics, schizophrenics, those suffering from hypertension or anxiety or those on heart medication or hormone treatments such as HRT or oral contraceptives. Take separately from vitamin B and C supplements. Avoid caffeine whilst taking this herb.

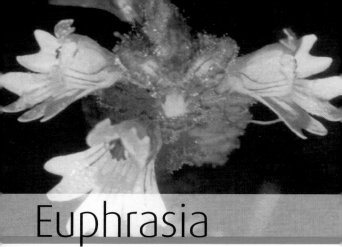

Euphrasia

Also known as:

Eyebright.

Uses:

Conjunctivitis, eye strain, hayfever.

Description:

Euphrasia is a small annual plant, native to Britain and Europe. It grows to a height of about 30cm and bears pale lilac flowers. It has been used as far back as the 17th Century for healthcare. Milton, in his poem 'Paradise Lost', describes how the Archangel Michael used 'Euphrasy' to clear Adam's sight.

How it works:

Euphrasia contains a number of active constituents, including aucubin, caffeic acid and tannins. This last group of compounds work as anti-inflammatory agents, helping to dry up secretions of the mucous membranes.

This is particularly relevant when we consider the most important role of Euphrasia — to reduce the inflammation of the delicate mucous membranes of the eyes (conjunctivitis) when they are afflicted by infections or allergy (hayfever). The preparation should be taken internally.

Additional advice:

Do not use Euphrasia externally.

Feverfew

Also known as:

Tanacetum parthenium.

Uses:

Migraine headaches.

Description:

Feverfew has daisy-like flowers, a characteristic of the Compositae family to which it belongs. It is a plant which is commonly found in temperate climes and, traditionally, those suffering from migraine headaches were advised to place a leaf from the feverfew plant in their sandwich!

How it works:

Feverfew has been subject to a fair amount of research. Sesquiterpene lactones are thought to be the main active constituents of the plant. They inhibit platelet aggregation and the secretion of serotonin, which is one of the substances released during a migraine headache.

Additional advice:

Some people may be prone to mouth ulcers when using Feverfew. Avoid if you have a known hypersensitivity to other members of the Compositae family such as Chamomile.

Galeopsis

Also known as:

Hemp Nettle.

Uses:

Stress incontinence, supportive treatment in asthma.

Description:

Hemp Nettle is a member of the Labiatae family, a group of plants commonly found in Germany.

How it works:

Galeopsis contains a large amount of silica, saponins and tannins. The silicic acid content increases non-specific lung resistance to allergies and pathogens through a temporary increase in white blood cells.

Silica is also of great importance in the regeneration of tissue. High concentrations are normally found in the trachea and lung tissue. Levels decrease with the presence of respiratory disease when the requirement becomes greater.

Saponins present have an expectorant action, which enhances the expulsion of phlegm from the lungs.

Galeopsis is also useful for stress incontinence and bedwetting through the astringent action of tannins in toning up tissue.

Additional advice:

Do not stop prescribed medication when using Galeopsis without the knowledge of your Doctor.

Alison Cullen

A qualified nutritional therapist, Alison has a busy practice in Ayrshire, Scotland.

"I have been using herbal remedies for many years and am constantly grateful for the healing properties of the plants available to us in Nature.

Some herbs are appropriate in acute situations to alleviate symptoms, whilst others can be used to tackle chronic ailments. In both situations I recommend herbs taken in the form of tinctures as, in my experience, these absorb faster and more effectively than other forms. The length of treatment depends on the condition and the constitution of the individual.

I trust that the information in this guide will assist in your healing process."

With the Compliments of Your Local Health Store:

ISBN 1-903379-11-3

9 781903 379110

VARICOSE ULCERS

Aesculus (Horse Chestnut)
Strengthens veins.

Echinacea
Speeds up wound healing and fights infection.

VARICOSE VEINS

Aesculus (Horse Chestnut)
Can be used short or long term to strengthen veins.

WATER RETENTION

Dandelion
Dandelion leaf is particularly effective at restoring water balance.

Solidago
Use this kidney toning herb if water retention is persistent.

Agnus castus
For hormonal water retention.

WIND

See FLATULENCE

WORMS

See INTESTINAL PARASITES

WOUND HEALING

Echinacea
Speeds up wound healing and fights infection.

Garlic

Also known as:
Allium sativum.

Uses:
High cholesterol, high blood pressure.

Description:
Garlic is one of the more commonly used health supplements in the world. It is said to be the world's second oldest medicine after Ephedra and is still one of the best and most popular herbal remedies. Remains of Garlic have been found in caves inhabited 10,000 years ago. A Sumerian clay tablet dating from 3,000 BC records the first Garlic prescription.

How it works:
It is now recognised that it is the ratio of the various types of cholesterol and fats in the blood which is more relevant than the totals measured. Whilst Garlic lowers the levels of cholesterol and triglycerides, it reduces the level of low density lipoproteins (LDL) whilst increasing the levels of high density lipoproteins (HDL). It has been suggested that an increase in HDL may enhance removal of cholesterol.

Garlic also has a mild action in lowering blood pressure and possesses antioxidant activity.

Additional advice:
No restrictions on use are known.

Ginger

Also known as:

Zingiber officinalis.

Uses:

Travel sickness, morning sickness, flatulence, poor circulation.

Description:

This is another example of how our food is also our medicine. The Ginger plant is native to South East Asia, where it is used extensively in cooking. A traditional food to fortify pregnant women in these countries is chicken soup heavily laced with Ginger.

How it works:

Ginger contains a number of substances, many of which are volatile oils. As a digestive tonic, Ginger improves the production and secretion of bile, aids fat breakdown and lowers blood cholesterol levels. This speeds up the digestive processes, allowing quicker transport of substances through the digestive tract, lessening the irritation in the intestines, reducing flatulence and intestinal spasms.

Additional advice:

Some people may experience heartburn or be sensitive to the taste of Ginger.

Ginkgo biloba

Also known as:

Memory Tree, Maidenhair Tree.

Uses:

Improves arterial circulation, cold hands and feet, Menière's Disease, chilblains, tinnitus, labyrinthitis, impotence, improves memory.

Description:

This is probably one of the oldest medicinal herbs known to Man. Its use can be traced to the oldest Chinese Materia Medica dating back to around 3,000 BC. Traditional Chinese medicine describes the ability of Ginkgo leaves to 'benefit the brain'. Today, Ginkgo extracts are among the most widely prescribed Phytomedicines in both Germany and France. In Germany alone, 10 million prescriptions for Ginkgo are written each year by more than 10,000 physicians.

How it works:

The action of Ginkgo has been quite clearly demonstrated in various research tests. Direct action on the arterial circulation increases the blood flow through these vessels. At the same time, the herb has been shown to inhibit a substance known as Platelet Activating Factor (PAF) which further improves blood flow whilst acting as an anti-inflammatory agent.

Ginkgo has also been shown to have anti-oxidant effects, which are important in stabilising cell membranes in the body.

Additional advice:

Consult a Healthcare Professional if using Aspirin or Warfarin.

Helianthus tuberosus

Also known as:

Jerusalem Artichoke.

Uses:

Weight control, appetite control, Syndrome X.

Description:

Despite its name, Jerusalem Artichoke is neither an artichoke nor from Jerusalem. It is native to North America and is a member of the sunflower family, sharing their ability to swivel around to follow the path of the sun. It is possible that it acquired the name 'Jerusalem' as a distortion of its Italian name 'Girasola', which means 'rotate towards the sun'.

How it works:

Jerusalem Artichoke slows down the rate at which sugars are broken down in the body. This means that your food will give you energy for a longer period of time, slowing down hunger pangs. Better metabolism of sugars also balances out swings in blood sugar levels, reducing sugar cravings that come when blood sugar levels drop.

Jerusalem Artichoke contains plant sugars that feed friendly bacteria in the gut, and these bacteria break down undigested food particles and prevent them from putrefying and causing embarrassing wind. As Jerusalem Artichoke also contains water soluble plant fibres, it helps to bulk up waste matters travelling through the colon and thus improves bowel regularity.

Additional advice:

No restrictions on use are known.

Hops

Also known as:

Humulus lupulus.

Uses:

Insomnia.

Description:

The plant Humulus is a climber which can be found in swamps and in the hedges of our cultivated gardens. Being an important ingredient in beer, it is extensively cultivated commercially. Hops has a long history of use in Phytotherapy. It was listed in the US Pharmacopoeia from 1831 to 1916 as a sedative.

How it works:

Hops contain substances known as humulones and lupulones. These are broken down in the body to substances which have a distinct sedative effect on the nervous system. This effect is extremely useful especially when combined with the herb Valerian, for insomnia, or when there is an element of nervous tension/anxiety involved.

Additional advice:

No restrictions on use are known.

Hypericum

Also known as:

St John's Wort.

Uses:

Depression, anxiety, SAD, neuralgia, sciatica, shingles.

Description:

This herb is the traditional remedy for depression. It is commonly found in temperate countries and has recently gained immense popularity as a herb used in healthcare.

How it works:

There is little doubt that Hypericum works by influencing the neurotransmitters in the brain. The substances responsible for this action are now known to be Hypericin and more recently, Hyperforin. However, it is widely accepted that the action of the herb cannot be assigned to a specific constituent but is rather the balanced effect of all the substances within the plant.

Hypericum has also been found to contain flavonoids which possess analgesic action in those suffering with neuralgia — the most common of which is sciatica.

Additional advice:

Please check with a Doctor/Pharmacist or Healthcare Professional if you are taking any prescribed medicines as Hypericum may affect the way they work.

Ivy

Also known as:

Hedera helix.

Uses:

Coughs, expectorant, mild bronchitis.

Description:

The Common Ivy is a plant which can be found easily in our gardens. It is a climbing plant and it is the leaves which are used medicinally.

How it works:

Ivy is an example of a herb which has an expectorant action on the chest, elicited by a reflex action in the stomach, due to its saponin content. It loosens the mucus from the tubes of the lungs, encouraging its expulsion and elimination. Often troublesome coughs indicate difficulty in eliminating mucus and a herb such as Ivy, in thinning mucus, helps to clear the chest.

The action of Ivy in this type of cough is enhanced particularly when Thyme is added.

Additional advice:

No restrictions on use are known.

Kelp

Also known as:

Macrocystis pyrifera.

Uses:

Stimulates metabolism, overweight, detoxification.

Description:

Kelp is a variety of seaweed, known to Botanists as the long-frond brown algae. It grows to lengths of up to 60 metres in the temperate parts of the Pacific and Atlantic Oceans. This plant used to play an important part in the culture of fishing communities where it was used for fuel and food. However, apart from Japan, the use of seaweed has faded out.

How it works:

Kelp is rich in iodine. It also contains bromine, trace elements and vitamin A. The main activity of Kelp lies with its iodine content. It is an important component of thyroid hormones, which play a major part in regulating the body's metabolism. Increasing the iodine available to the body will increase the level of activity in the thyroid gland, raising the body's general metabolism. Kelp also contains substances known as alginates. These molecules have the unique property of being able to absorb onto the surfaces of heavy metals, radioactive substances and organic molecules such as cholesterol.

Additional advice:

Kelp is not advised for anyone with high blood pressure, kidney disorders or thyroid conditions, unless taken under medical supervision. Certain people may also be allergic to iodine, and hence, Kelp. Do not use if pregnant or breastfeeding.

Knotgrass

Also known as:
Polygonum aviculare.

Uses:
Arthritis, gout, Carpal Tunnel Syndrome, lumbago.

Description:
Knotgrass is one of the oldest traditional remedies for arthritis and general inflammatory joint conditions.

It appears as a weed in many temperate countries and is difficult to eradicate once established, due to its strong root and runner system below soil level.

How it works:
The active substances of this plant have not yet been studied extensively. Knotgrass is known to contain silica, which can help to improve the elasticity and strength of connective tissues in the body and particularly the joints.

In addition, the plant appears to work as an anti-inflammatory agent by helping the body in the elimination of toxins.

Additional advice:
No restrictions on use are known.

Linseed

Also known as:

Semen linum.

Uses:

Laxative.

Description:

Linseed is the seed from the plant known as Common Flax (Linum usitatissimum). In the past, flax played a very important part in the economy and culture of communities in which it was grown.

How it works:

Linseed contains about 5% mucilage, 40% oil and 20% protein.

Although seemingly least important, it is the mucilage action which endows Linseed with a unique property.

In the presence of water, mucilage has the ability to swell, increasing its volume considerably. This 'bulking' ability can be extremely beneficial to the digestive tract when bowel action is slow or 'lazy'. The bulking action relies on water, and hence Linseed should be taken with plenty of fluid.

The oils present in Linseed also act as a lubricant, supporting the bulking action of mucilage.

Additional advice:

It is not advisable to use laxative agents on a long term basis without the advice of a Healthcare Professional.

Luffa

Also known as:

Sponge cucumber.

Uses:

Used as part of a programme for reducing allergic reactions such as sneezing, itchy and runny eyes and nose, blocked or stuffy nose, wheezy chest, etc. Hayfever and other forms of allergic rhinitis respond well.

Description:

This tropical plant is used with a variety of others to combat the symptoms of allergies, particularly those with hayfever-like effects.

The benefit of using this type of natural remedy is that it has none of the side effects common with conventional antihistamine-type medications, such as drowsiness, fatigue and dependency. It can be used long or short term, and is suitable for those sensitive to chemical medications.

How it works:

There is very little research available to help us with our understanding of the action of this plant. Empirical evidence indicates its effectiveness, but as yet we have no clear picture of the mechanisms of action.

Additional advice:

No restrictions on use are known.

Marum verum

Also known as:

Cat's Thyme.

Use:

Snoring, nasal polyps.

Description:

Marum verum is a small shrub, native to Spain. Its traditional use has been in the form of snuff. The fresh leaves and young branches, when rubbed, give off an aromatic smell that can trigger sneezing.

How it works:

The evidence of Marum verum's activity is mainly empirical and derived from clinical experience. It appears to have the ability to reduce inflammation of the nasal passages.

Its ability to reduce snoring could be due to the removal of blockages and better functioning of tissues, membranes and nervous pathways in the nose and throat.

Additional advice:

Do not use if pregnant or breastfeeding.

Milk Thistle

Also known as:

Carduus marianus, Silybum marianum.

Uses:

Liver function stimulant, detoxification, liver tonic, psoriasis, alopecia.

Description:

The Milk Thistle is a large plant with glossy, green, spiky leaves bearing conspicuous white veins. The flowers are purple and large.

The plant originates from the Mediterranean and it is now cultivated in many parts of Europe as an ornamental plant. Milk Thistle has a long history of use as a medicinal plant.

It was previously administered for its bitter properties, but more recently it has been recognised more and more as an excellent remedy for liver complaints.

How it works:

The main constituent of Milk Thistle appears to be the substance known as silymarin. This has the unique function of being able to act directly on the cells of the liver producing a liver-protective effect.

Silymarin has been shown to be able to prevent liver cell damage, through stimulating the enzymatic function of liver cells and encouraging the regeneration of the liver.

All these factors are important in overall health, with the liver acting as the most important avenue for the elimination of toxins found within the body.

Additional advice:

Medical opinion should be sought when acute or chronic liver conditions are present.

Neem

Also known as:

Azadirachta indica.

Uses:

Mild skin infections, psoriasis, eczema, athlete's foot, ringworm, head lice.

Description:

The Neem tree is a member of the mahogany family, originating from the Bay of Bengal. It has been used traditionally for the treatment of many diseases in Ayurvedic medicine and for the protection of people and animals from insect pests.

How it works:

The Neem tree contains at least 35 biologically active principles distributed throughout the leaves, seeds and bark.

Neem leaves have antibacterial activity, the constituents nimbolide and nimbic acid have been shown to be active against the bacteria responsible for abscesses and wound infections. In addition, the leaves and the oil from the seeds have anti-inflammatory properties.

The insecticidal properties of Neem oil are due to the constituent Azadirachtin A. It mimics the insect hormonal system and affects feeding, development and reproduction.

Additional advice:

Neem should not be taken internally. Diabetics should not self treat any conditions of the foot. Do not use if pregnant or breastfeeding.

Papaya

Also known as:

Carica papaya.

Uses:

Indigestion, incomplete digestion, intestinal parasites.

Description:

The Papaya tree, native to Taiwan, reaches heights of up to 10 metres, and has large, long stemmed leaves and fruit rather like small melons. The leaf of the Papaya tree, as well as its fruit, has a long tradition of use in Asia for digestive problems. The fruit is sweet in taste and now popular in Western countries.

How it works:

The leaf and fruit of the Papaya tree contain protein-digesting enzymes (papain and chymopapain), which help to break down proteins, carbohydrates and fats. Papaya leaves are actually used commercially to tenderise meat, due to their enzymatic activity. In the human body, papain has a similar action to the digestive enzyme pepsin, which should be produced in the stomach. In those with impaired or weak digestive function, papaya may therefore assist in the proper breakdown of food.

Papain has been shown to dissolve the outer cuticle of intestinal worms, making it a useful tool in their removal.

Additional advice:

Those with chronic intestinal tract diseases should consult a Healthcare Professional before using this remedy.

Passiflora

Also known as:

Passion Flower.

Uses:

Anxiety, nervous tension, nerve pain, depression, nervous exhaustion.

Description:

Passiflora is a climbing plant, popular in gardens in Europe. It originates from South America and the East Indies and was traditionally used as a nerve tonic in neuralgia. It is used extensively in Homoeopathy.

How it works:

Passiflora has a sedative effect on the central nervous system. However, its mode of action is not clear and the active constituents in the plant have not been clearly identified. It was originally thought that the active constituent was the alkaloid known as passiflorine or Harman.

Additional advice:

Avoid excessive doses. Do not use if pregnant or breastfeeding.

Peppermint

Also known as:

Mentha piperita.

Uses:

Irritable Bowel Syndrome (IBS).

Description:

There are many varieties of Peppermint which can be found. These differ in their medicinal properties, as a result of differing levels of volatile oils.

How it works:

Menthol is one of the most prominent of the volatile oils found in Peppermint. The plant as a whole works as a carminative (dispels wind), reducing the symptoms of nausea, colic, bloating and wind. It also relaxes muscle tension in the colon which helps to relieve spasms.

Research has shown that Peppermint is able to relieve the symptoms of Irritable Bowel Syndrome.

Additional advice:

No restrictions on use are known.

Petasites

Also known as:

Butterbur.

Uses:

Migraine headaches, muscle spasm, period pain, gastric pain, lumbago, neuralgia, shingles.

Description:

Butterbur is a member of the daisy family, commonly found in damp woodland areas or growing along riverbanks. The leaves of the plant are very large and round, hence the name Petasites, meaning 'large brimmed hat'.

How it works:

Petasites contains the constituent petasin. This is thought to be the most important active ingredient due to its antispasmodic and pain relieving properties.

Research has shown that these properties are particularly useful both for the treatment and prevention of migraine.

Recent research also suggests that Petasites is useful for the treatment of hayfever and other forms of allergic rhinitis.

Additional advice:

Petasites should not be used to treat migraine symptoms that have not been previously diagnosed by a Healthcare Professional.

If you are using this product long term, a two week break in treatment is recommended every eight weeks.

Plantago

Also known as:

Plantago lanceolata, Ribwort Plantain.

Uses:

Ear infections, glue ear, upper respiratory tract congestion, catarrh, tinnitus.

Description:

This is a very common plant in Europe, growing in large quantities in dry meadows and fields, where it is easy to find. Plantago, a member of the Plantain family, produces a rosette of slender pointed leaves and a flowering stem which arises from the centre, carrying small flowers.

How it works:

Plantago contains mucilage, tannins and silicic acid. It is probably the mucilage which contributes most to the action of the plant as a cough remedy.

Plantago also has the ability to reduce the amount of inflammation present in the mucous membranes of the upper respiratory tract.

It has been noted that plantain juice will not go mouldy during storage, although large amounts of sugar are present. It has been found that this is due to the presence of naturally occurring antibiotics. This may explain its action in conditions such as middle ear infections and glue ear.

Additional advice:

No restrictions on use are known.

Propolis

Uses:

Cold sores.

Description:

Propolis has been used as a medicine for more than 2,000 years.

Bees make propolis from plant exudates for the protection and sterilisation of their hives. The exudates are mixed by the bees with beeswax, to make a paste that can be smoothed over the inside of the hive, making it more secure and simultaneously providing an antiseptic coating, reducing the growth of bacteria, viruses and moulds inside the hive. Mankind has adapted this useful material to his own medical needs.

How it works:

Propolis is rich in amino acids, trace elements and flavonoids, which work synergistically to provide the antiseptic, antibacterial and antifungal effect.

In the case of cold sores, propolis inactivates the Herpes Simplex virus (responsible for cold sores), stopping it from replicating and at the same time reducing the likelihood of bacterial infection around the site of the cold sore. Its local anaesthetic action means the cold sore will be less painful, and studies have shown that healing time can be cut by as much as 50%.

Additional advice:

Do not use if allergic to bee products.

Sage

Also known as:

Salvia officinalis.

Uses:

Menopausal hot flushes, sore throats.

Description:

Sage is commonly used to enhance the taste of food. The plant is native to the Mediterranean, although it also grows well in temperate climes.

How it works:

Sage is one of the plants known as a phyto-oestrogen. In itself, the plant does not contain any oestrogen-like compounds but possesses the potential of influencing oestrogen activity in the body.

In addition, Sage has a separate role in preventing sweating. The combination of these two actions makes Sage an excellent preparation to help with the hot flushes which often accompany the decline in hormonal levels at the time of the menopause.

Sage has also been found to possess antibacterial properties and can be very beneficial for sore throats when used as a gargle.

Additional advice:

Consult a Healthcare Professional before use if you are taking oral contraceptives, HRT or Tamoxifen or if you suffer from diabetes or epilepsy.

Saw Palmetto

Also known as:

Sabal serrulata, Serenoa repens.

Uses:

Enlarged prostate, Benign Prostatic Hypertrophy, alopecia, impotence.

Description:

This is a small palm with fan-shaped leaves. The fruit, which is dark red, is the size of an olive and contains a volatile oil known as palmetto oil. It is the fruit that is used medicinally.

Saw Palmetto is considered by herbalists to be the prime remedy for prostate problems.

How it works:

The condition of an enlarged prostate is commonly found in men over the age of 50. This enlargement is the result of the cells in the prostate becoming more sensitive to circulating hormonal levels in the body. Cells of the prostate enlarge, which in turn cause the whole gland to increase in size.

Saw Palmetto inhibits enzymes at the level of the prostate cells, reducing the action of hormones. This is a local effect, confined to the prostate gland.

Additional advice:

Medical advice should be sought if the condition persists or is accompanied by bleeding or a fever.

Solidago

Also known as:

Golden Rod.

Uses:

Diuretic, water retention, improves renal function, kidney tonic.

Description:

The herb Solidago is a traditional kidney tonic. It is a small, herbaceous plant found in temperate countries and often found in the natural flora of grassy mountainous areas.

How it works:

Whilst Solidago has diuretic action, this is not the prime role of the plant. Solidago has been shown to have important anti-inflammatory, antispasmodic and antiseptic action and seems to strengthen kidney function.

This makes it useful as an agent to counter inflammation and irritation of the kidneys, when infection or stones are present. The diuretic action is also useful in helping to dissolve kidney stones.

Additional advice:

Consult a Doctor if the urinary tract condition persists or if accompanied by bleeding, fever, nausea or vomiting.

Spilanthes

Also known as:

Paracress.

Uses:

Athlete's foot, ringworm, oral thrush, candidiasis, thrush.

Description:

Spilanthes originates from South America and grows in wet, damp places in temperate climates. It is a member of the Asteraceae family and was traditionally used in Europe for the external treatment of fungal skin infections.

How it works:

Spilanthes contains the essential oil spilanthole which is anti-inflammatory.

Studies carried out in the 1950s highlighted the insecticidal properties of the essential oil. Spilanthes also contains tannic acid, a known astringent.

Recent research has confirmed the antifungal activity of Spilanthes, especially against the Trichophyton species responsible for athlete's foot infections.

Additional advice:

Do not use if pregnant or breastfeeding.

Thyme

Also known as:

Thymus vulgaris, Common Thyme.

Uses:

Chest conditions, e.g. mild bronchitis, coughs.

Description:

This is another herb which is well known for its culinary use. There are many species of Thyme. Common Thyme originates from the Mediterranean and is the most widely used medicinal variety.

How it works:

The primary active components of Thyme are the volatile oils, especially thymol. These act locally on the lungs as they are eliminated from the body through the respiratory tract, disinfecting the airways, relaxing bronchial spasm and reducing the viscosity of mucus.

These actions help the lungs expel mucus, benefiting bronchitis and chesty catarrhal conditions.

Additional advice:

Consult a Doctor if blood is present in mucus.

Tormentil

Also known as:

Potentilla tormentilla, Bloodroot.

Uses:

Diarrhoea, bowel inflammation, IBS, colitis, Crohn's Disease, diverticultis, intestinal parasites.

Description:

The Tormentil herb is a member of the Rose family. It can be found all over Europe, growing wild in woods, moors and grassy pieces of ground. It is a small plant with yellow flowers. The root is thick and red on the inside, giving rise to the name 'Bloodroot'.

How it works:

Tormentil has a high tannin content, which gives it a distinct astringent action on the digestive tract. Tannins bind to the proteins present in the irritated lining of the bowel, forming a layer which soothes and, at the same time, provides a barrier against infective organisms and toxins. They also slow down the frequency of bowel motions, encouraging the healing of an inflamed bowel.

Additional advice:

Consult a Doctor or Practitioner if acute diarrhoea persists for more than 36 hours.

Urtica

Also known as:

Stinging Nettle.

Uses:

Arthritis, rheumatoid arthritis, gout, detoxification, allergic rashes, prickly heat.

Description:

Urtica is the name of the Stinging Nettle commonly encountered on wasteland as a weed. It has, however, been treasured for a long time by herbalists as an excellent blood tonic.

How it works:

Nettle has a diuretic action, attributed to flavonoids which increase the excretion of a number of waste substances from the body, particularly the acid metabolites. This action is of particular benefit in gout and arthritic conditions.

Urtica has a nutritive value, containing vitamin C, iron, calcium, potassium and silica, which explains its tonic action.

Additional advice:

Do not use if suffering from diabetes or blood pressure problems.

Uva-ursi

Also known as:

Arctostaphylos uva-ursi, Bearberry.

Uses:

Cystitis, urinary tract infections.

Description:

Uva-ursi is a small plant found in Europe. It has small peculiarly-shaped flowers, which some consider to resemble a bladder.

How it works:

Uva-ursi has urinary antiseptic properties by virtue of a glycoside known as arbutin. The way this substance works in urinary tract infection is unique.

Arbutin is absorbed by the body and broken down to hydroquinone and glucose. Hydroquinone is then excreted in the urine, where it exerts a direct antiseptic action in the kidneys and bladder. This action is stronger in alkaline urine so a fruit and vegetable based diet is recommended.

Additional advice:

Consult a Healthcare Professional if symptoms persist for more than one week. Do not use if pregnant or breastfeeding.

Valerian

Also known as:

Valeriana officinalis.

Uses:

Anxiety, nervous tension, stress, insomnia.

Description:

This is a herb which is widely found across Europe. It is one of the oldest herbs in use and has been the subject of extensive research.

How it works:

The tranquillising action of Valerian has been attributed to a number of components. The group of compounds known as valepotriates have the ability to calm the nerves.

The substance valerenic acid inhibits the breakdown of GABA, a chemical transmitter in the brain, which helps to decrease activity in the nervous system, and this in turn can aid the promotion of sleep.

In addition, a number of other constituents in Valerian have been shown to possess antispasmodic activity on muscles.

Additional advice:

Consult a Doctor or Practitioner if currently using other medicines for the nerves.

Vinca minor

Also known as:

Lesser Periwinkle.

Uses:

Impaired memory, tinnitus, Menière's Disease, poor circulation, cold hands and feet, chilblains, nosebleeds.

Description:

Vinca minor is a perennial plant and a common inhabitant of woods and hedgerows. It was used historically for fluxes — bleeding at the mouth or nose, and for bleeding piles.

How it works:

Vinca minor contains the alkaloid vincamine in its leaves, which has an astringent effect on the tissues. Vinca minor works via its astringent/tonic effect on blood vessel tone throughout the body. Blood supply to the brain is improved helping memory, concentration and the alleviation of dizziness, making Vinca minor an alternative when Ginkgo biloba is contraindicated.

Additional advice:

People with brain tumours should not use this herb. Do not use if pregnant or breastfeeding.

Viola tricolor

Also known as:

Wild Pansy.

Uses:

Eczema, non-specific skin rashes, acne.

Description:

This is another plant that is familiar to many people. Not many know, however, that herbalists have for many years taken advantage of its distinct action on the skin to help with eczema and other skin rashes.

How it works:

Viola contains saponins. These soap-like molecules are able to soothe inflamed areas of skin and, in part, are responsible for the soothing effect of the herb when applied externally.

The saponin content also makes Viola an eliminative remedy. Blood flow to the kidneys is enhanced as is the elimination of toxins.

Viola also contains high levels of flavonoids which have the ability to stabalise capillary membranes. This is an important consideration in inflammatory conditions of the skin.

Additional advice:

Do not use if pregnant or breastfeeding.

Yarrow

Also known as:

Achillea millefolium.

Uses:

Indigestion, digestive tonic, food intolerances, leaky gut, flatulence, bloating.

Description:

Yarrow is classified by herbalists as one of the bitter herbs. Other herbs in this category include Centaurium, Gentian and Dandelion. These have the common ability to stimulate digestive processes, increasing gastric juice secretion and improving the breakdown of food.

How it works:

Yarrow contains volatile oils and flavonoids. These have an antispasmodic and anti-inflammatory action on the digestive system, easing colic and reducing flatulence.

Bitters stimulate the tastebuds. This triggers off a reflex nerve action which increases the flow of saliva and stomach enzymes. The sum total of this is an improvement in the digestive function of the stomach and small intestines.

Bitters can also be very useful for children with poor appetites.

Additional advice:

Do not use if you intend to sunbathe or use a sunbed as Yarrow can have a photosensitising action.

Section Two
Herbs
for Health

ACID STOMACH

Centaurium
Take 15 minutes before meals, in a little water. Hold in mouth before swallowing. The bitter taste is necessary for the beneficial action.

Yarrow
Take 5-10 minutes before food. Best taken in combination with stomach bitters such as Centaurium, and other soothing, antispasmodic herbs such as Melissa (Lemon Balm).

ACNE

Echinacea
Well known for its positive effect on the skin. Use Echinacea tincture internally and apply Echinacea cream externally.

Agnus castus
If acne relates to the menstrual cycle or puberty (in both sexes).

Viola tricolor
Very gentle and appropriate for all ages. Condition may worsen before improving.

ALLERGIC RHINITIS

Luffa
Also known as Sponge Cucumber, this tropical plant can be found in combination with other plants to help alleviate the symptoms of hayfever and allergic rhinitis. Take for several weeks before and throughout the hayfever season.

Echinacea/Devil's Claw
Either of these remedies can be used long term to strengthen the immune system against allergic reactions.

ALOPECIA: in men

Saw Palmetto
Thought to have a rebalancing effect on hormone levels.

Milk Thistle
Improving liver function may aid hair keratinisation.

ALOPECIA: in women

Milk Thistle
Improving liver function may aid hair keratinisation.

Urtica (Stinging Nettle)
A source of iron and a blood tonic.

ALZHEIMER'S DISEASE

Ginkgo biloba
May be used protectively as well as to arrest development of condition.

ANAEMIA

Urtica (Stinging Nettle)
A source of iron and a blood tonic. Suitable for long term use.

ANOREXIA

Centaurium
Take 15 minutes before meals, in a little water. Hold in the mouth before swallowing. The bitter taste is necessary for the beneficial action.

ANXIETY

Avena sativa
A gentle, mild herb, suitable for daytime use and for children.

Valerian
Use a low dose during the day for remaining calm. Take a higher dose at night to aid sleep.

Hypericum (St John's Wort)
Mixed with soothing herbs such as Melissa (Lemon Balm), it can address the low moods that can accompany stress and anxiety.

Passiflora
Gently calming for states of depression combined with anxiety.

APPETITE LOSS

Centaurium
Take 15 minutes before meals, in a little water. Hold in the mouth before swallowing. The bitter taste is necessary for the beneficial action.

ARTHRITIS — osteo

Devil's Claw
A powerful anti-inflammatory for pain relief. No contraindications with other medication. Suitable for long term use. Does not affect the stomach.

Arnica
Now shown to possess strong anti-inflammatory properties. For external use only.

Knotgrass
Breaks down knotty deposits in joints. Take for at least four months.

ARTHRITIS — rheumatoid

Devil's Claw
A powerful anti-inflammatory for pain relief. No contraindications with other medication. Suitable for long term use. Does not affect the stomach.

Arnica
Now shown to possess strong anti-inflammatory properties. For external use only.

Urtica (Stinging Nettle)
A source of iron and a blood tonic. Suitable for long term use. Removes uric acid deposits from tissues and joints — very useful in arthritic conditions.

ASTHMA

Galeopsis
Take for at least six months to help strengthen lung tissue.

Echinacea
Immune-boosting action to reduce risk of infection.

ATHLETE'S FOOT

Spilanthes
Antifungal herb to be taken internally and applied externally.

Neem
Both the leaf and oil have antifungal properties. For external use only.

BLOATING

Yarrow
Take 5-10 minutes before food. Best taken in combination with stomach bitters such as Centaurium, and other soothing, antispasmodic herbs such as Melissa (Lemon Balm).

BLOOD PRESSURE

Crataegus (Hawthorn)
Balances blood pressure, whether high or low. Take for at least six months to judge effect.

Garlic
A blood purifier that cleanses arterial walls to improve blood flow.

BPH (Benign Prostatic Hypertrophy)

Saw Palmetto
Anti-inflammatory effect on prostate gland tissue.

BRONCHITIS — mild

Ivy
Antispasmodic (stops hacking coughs) and loosens mucus.

Thyme
Disinfects airways, relaxes bronchial tubes and thins mucus.

White Horehound
Helps lungs expel mucus.

Echinacea
If infection is present.

CANDIDA

Spilanthes
Antifungal herb to be taken internally.

Echinacea
Antifungal and strengthens immune response.

CARPAL TUNNEL SYNDROME

Knotgrass
Anti-inflammatory and cleansing properties.

CATARRH

Plantago
Clears ear/nose/throat tract.

Echinacea
Helps body to fight infection.

Berberis
Use for its anti-inflammatory properties.

CHILBLAINS

Ginkgo biloba
Stimulates circulation to extremities.

Vinca minor
Improves arterial circulation.

CHOLESTEROL

Globe Artichoke
Lowers cholesterol and lipid levels in the blood.

Garlic
Blood purifier, helping to prevent cholesterol build up.

CHRONIC FATIGUE SYNDROME

Echinacea
Antiviral.

Ginkgo biloba
Improves delivery of nutrients to all organs of the body.

Eleutherococcus (Siberian Ginseng)
Boosts immune system and increases energy.

CIRCULATION — poor

Ginkgo biloba
Improves blood supply to extremities.

Ginger
Warming blood tonic that boosts circulation.

Vinca minor
Increases tone of blood vessels.

COLD HANDS AND FEET
See CIRCULATION

COLD SORES

Hypericum (St John's Wort)
Antiviral action. Especially appropriate for nervous system.

Echinacea
Internally as tincture and externally as cream. Antiviral and immune system boosting.

Propolis
A well-known remedy with antiviral, anti-inflammatory and wound healing properties.

COLITIS — ulcerative

Tormentil
In tincture form, works fast to stop diarrhoea. Take longer term to help heal intestinal lining.

Echinacea
Boosts immunity and clears infection.

Berberis
Use for its anti-inflammatory properties.

Additional advice: There are many dietary aspects to this ailment — consult a qualified Nutritionist for more information.

COLITIS — non specific

Tormentil
In tincture format, works fast to stop diarrhoea. Take longer term to help heal intestinal lining.

Additional advice: Food allergies and intolerances are often involved — consult a qualified Nutritionist for advice.

COMMON COLD

Echinacea
Take in tincture form for swift effect on existing colds. Taken in a maintenance dose throughout the winter, it often prevents colds from occurring.

CONJUNCTIVITIS — allergic

Luffa
If allergic reaction is seasonal, take prior to and throughout allergy season. Reduces allergic reaction, especially in the eyes and nose.

Devil's Claw
Taken long term, will help rebalance immune system.

CONJUNCTIVITIS — infective

Echinacea
Anti-infective.

Euphrasia
Use internally to ease inflamed, sore eyes quickly.

CONSTIPATION

Psyllium husks
Soaked in water or juice, these can soften and bulk the stool, making it easier to pass.

Senna
A strong laxative, for short term use only.

Linseeds
Soak a tablespoonful overnight in water and add to breakfast cereal.

CONVALESCENCE

Eleutherococcus (Siberian Ginseng)
Enables the body to adapt to challenging circumstances and boosts energy levels. Ideal for short term use after illness.

COUGHS

Ivy
Antispasmodic (stops hacking coughs) and loosens mucus.

Thyme
Disinfects airways, relaxes bronchial tubes and thins mucus.

White Horehound
Helps lungs expel mucus.

CROHN'S DISEASE

Tormentil
Stops diarrhoea quickly and aids healing of intestinal lining.

Devil's Claw
Anti-inflammatory and rebalances immune system when used long term.

Berberis
Use for its anti-inflammatory properties.

CYSTITIS

Uva-ursi
Disinfects the bladder and helps to heal the lining of the urinary tract.

Echinacea
Boosts immunity and clears infection.

DEPRESSION

Hypericum (St John's Wort)
Clinical trials have shown this herb to be excellent for mild to moderate depression. Tincture format gives speedy results, but allow one to four weeks for full effect. (Severe or ongoing depression must always be treated by a Healthcare Professional.)

Passiflora
Gently calming for states of depression combined with anxiety.

DETOXIFICATION

Milk Thistle
Tones and cleanses the liver.

Solidago
Cleansing for the kidneys.

Calendula
Cleansing action on the lymphatic system.

Linseeds
Helps bowel movements. Soak a tablespoon overnight in water and add to breakfast cereal.

DIARRHOEA

Tormentil
Stops diarrhoea quickly.

DIVERTICULITIS

Tormentil
Stops diarrhoea quickly.

Psyllium husks
Soaked in water or juice, these can soften and bulk the stool, making it easier to pass.

Echinacea
Anti-infective.

DYSMENORRHOEA
See PERIOD PAIN

EARACHE glue ear, middle ear infections (otitis media)

Plantago
Clears catarrh from ear/nose/throat tract. Avoiding dairy products will speed up decongestion.

Echinacea
Anti-infective.

ECZEMA

Viola tricolor
Especially useful for childhood eczema. Skin nourishing. Condition may get worse temporarily before clearing up.

Neem
Has anti-inflammatory properties. For external use only.

Additional advice: There are often food allergies involved and many nutrients will help. A qualified Nutritionist will be able to advise you.

EYE STRAIN

Euphrasia
For swift, short term relief from tired, strained, sore eyes. Use internally only.

Bilberry
Long term protection against all forms of degenerative eye disease and eye strain. Take for several months to strengthen eyes if exposed to long periods of computer work, reading or driving.

FATIGUE

Eleutherococcus (Siberian Ginseng)
Excellent short term help for energy slumps.

FIBROIDS

Agnus castus
Helps increase progesterone levels. Take for four to six months to see results.

FIBROMYALGIA

Devil's Claw
Strong but gentle anti-inflammatory action.

Arnica
Now shown to possess strong anti-inflammatory properties. For external use only.

FLATULENCE

Peppermint
Antispasmodic and calming.

Ginger
Take as tincture, drink as tea or eat in foods.

FLU

Echinacea
Take in tincture form for swift effect on existing colds and flu. Taken in maintenance dose throughout the winter, it often prevents them occurring.

FOOD INTOLERANCES

Yarrow
Take 5-10 minutes before food. Best taken in combination with stomach bitters such as Centaurium, and other soothing, antispasmodic herbs such as Melissa (Lemon Balm).

Centaurium
Take 15 minutes before meals, in a little water. Hold in the mouth before swallowing. The bitter taste is necessary for the beneficial action.

FRACTURES

Urtica (Stinging Nettle)
A source of calcium and a useful blood tonic.

GALLSTONES

Globe Artichoke
Reduces lipid and cholesterol levels in the blood. Assists in metabolism of fats.

Dandelion
A splendid liver tonic, ideal for resolving and protecting against gallstones.

Berberis
This herb is multi-functional, toning the whole digestive system. It is also anti-infective, boosting spleen function.

GASTRITIS

Yarrow
Take 5-10 minutes before food. Best taken in combination with stomach bitters such as Centaurium, and other soothing, antispasmodic herbs such as Melissa (Lemon Balm).

Peppermint
Antispasmodic and calming for the digestive tract.

Petasites
Antispasmodic in gastric disturbances. Excellent pain relief.

Additional advice: All stomach bitters, such as Centaurium and Gentian, will be helpful for both prevention and relief in these circumstances.

GLUE EAR

See EARACHE

GOUT

Urtica (Stinging Nettle)
Removes uric acid from the system. A blood tonic.

Knotgrass
Breaks down calcified deposits and removes them from the tissues.
Take for several months for best effect.

HAEMORRHOIDS

Aesculus (Horse Chestnut)
Use long term to strengthen veins throughout the body. Follow advice
for CONSTIPATION.

HAYFEVER

Luffa
Also known as Sponge Cucumber, this tropical plant can be found
in combination with other plants that alleviate the symptoms of
hayfever and allergic rhinitis. Take for several weeks before and
throughout the hayfever season.

Euphrasia
Short term relief for itchy, irritated eyes. Use internally.

Echinacea/Devil's Claw
Either of these remedies can be used long term to strengthen the
immune system against allergic reactions such as hayfever.

HEADACHES

Petasites
Antispasmodic for migraine-type or tension-induced headaches.

Feverfew
Can protect against migraine headaches if taken daily.

Additional advice: If headaches are mainly stress-induced, use herbs
listed under STRESS.

HEAD LICE

Neem
Has anti-insecticidal properties.

HEARTBURN

Centaurium
Take 15 minutes before meals, in a little water. Hold in the mouth before
swallowing. The bitter taste is necessary for the beneficial action.

HERPES

See COLD SORES

HIATUS HERNIA

Centaurium
Take 15 minutes before meals, in a little water. Hold in mouth before swallowing. The bitter taste is necessary for the beneficial action.

HIGH BLOOD PRESSURE

Crataegus (Hawthorn)
Taken for six months, will gently ameliorate the condition.

Garlic
Helps to clear arteries, to reduce blood pressure.

Passiflora
A remedy against hypertensive stress.

HOT FLUSHES

Salvia (Sage)
Works for sweaty palms and feet, as well as menopausal flushes and sweats. Urtica (Stinging Nettle), taken alongside this herb, may increase the effect.

Black Cohosh
Phyto-oestrogenic. May improve sweats, reduce aches and pains and increase libido. Do not use if suffering from breast cancer.

HYPERACTIVITY

Avena sativa
Particularly suitable for children.

IBS (Irritable Bowel Syndrome)

Tormentil
Reduces intestinal spasm, stops diarrhoea and promotes healing of intestinal lining.

Peppermint
Antispasmodic and calming for the digestive tract.

Psyllium husks
Soaked in water or juice, these can soften and bulk the stool, making it easier to pass.

Additional advice: Many foods can exacerbate symptoms. Stress is often a trigger. Consider stress management options and take dietary advice.

IMMUNE SYSTEM

Echinacea
Immunomodulator. Rebalances the immune system.

IMPOTENCE

Saw Palmetto
Restores prostate function, having a positive effect on the libido.

Ginkgo biloba
Improves peripheral circulation.

Avena sativa
A remedy made from oats, a traditional aphrodisiac.

Additional advice: Impotence can be a side effect of many medical drugs. Check with a Doctor.

INCONTINENCE — men

Saw Palmetto
Reduces prostate problems, improving urine flow.

INCONTINENCE — women

Galeopsis
Take for six months to strengthen pelvic floor.

INDIGESTION

Centaurium
Take 15 minutes before meals, in a little water. Hold in the mouth before swallowing. The bitter taste is necessary for the beneficial action.

Yarrow
Take 5-10 minutes before food. Best taken in combination with stomach bitters such as Centaurium, and other soothing, antispasmodic herbs such as Melissa (Lemon Balm).

Peppermint
Antispasmodic and calming for the digestive tract.

INFECTIONS

Echinacea
Anti-infective.

INSOMNIA

Valerian
Can be used during the day to reduce stress build up, or just at night to aid sleep.

Hops
For a sedative effect on the central nervous system.

Passiflora
Calms the nervous system, relaxing muscles and releasing tension. Improves sleep quality.

INTESTINAL PARASITES

Papaya
Tropical fruit well known in the East. Contains useful digestive enzymes.

Tormentil
Astringent action helps dispel parasites.

KIDNEY INFECTION — mild

Solidago
A kidney tonic, disinfecting and soothing the kidneys.

Echinacea
Anti-infective.

LABYRINTHITIS

Ginkgo biloba
Improves blood supply to the head.

Echinacea
Anti-infective.

LARYNGITIS

Echinacea
Anti-infective.

LEAKY GUT

Yarrow
To soothe inflammation and improve absorption.

Devil's Claw
Anti-inflammatory and can reduce allergic reactions.

LIVER DISORDERS

Milk Thistle
Encourages the regeneration of liver cells and protects them from damage.

Dandelion
An excellent, cleansing liver tonic.

Artichoke
Improves fat metabolism, reducing lipid and cholesterol levels.

LUMBAGO

Petasites
Possesses antispasmodic properties and is excellent for pain relief.

Devil's Claw
Anti-inflammatory and pain relieving.

Knotgrass
Dissolves calcified deposits. Needs to be taken for several months.

MEMORY — poor

Ginkgo biloba
Improves blood supply to brain.

Vinca minor
Increases tone of blood vessels, improving circulation.

MENIÈRE'S DISEASE

Vinca minor
Increases tone of blood vessels.

Ginkgo biloba
Improves arterial blood supply.

MENOPAUSE

There are many symptoms and many remedies. It may be necessary to try different remedies or combinations of remedies to suit your individual circumstances.

Salvia (Sage)
A specific remedy for hot flushes and night sweats.

Black Cohosh
Phyto-oestrogenic. May improve sweats, reduce aches and pains and increase libido. Do not use if suffering from breast cancer.

Passiflora
Gently calming for states of depression combined with anxiety.

Eleutherococcus (Siberian Ginseng)
Balances hormone levels. Improves energy levels and libido.

Hypericum (St John's Wort)
Lifts spirits, easing temporary depression and sleeping problems.

Ginkgo biloba
Improves memory.

MIDDLE EAR INFECTIONS

See EARACHE

MIGRAINE

Petasites
Antispasmodic pain relief.

Feverfew
Taken daily, can prevent migraines occurring.

MORNING SICKNESS

Ginger
Take as tincture, drink as tea or eat in foods.

MOTION SICKNESS

See TRAVEL SICKNESS

MUSCLE SPASM

Petasites
Possesses antispasmodic properties and is excellent for pain relief.

NASAL POLYPS

Marum verum
Restorative for the tissues of the nasal passage.

NERVE PAIN

See NEURALGIA

NERVOUS EXHAUSTION

Avena sativa
A gentle, nourishing sedative.

Hypericum (St John's Wort)
Antidepressant and improves sleep.

Passiflora
Calms the nervous system, relaxing muscles and releasing tension.

NERVOUS TENSION

Hypericum
Improves stress symptoms such as nervous tension, anxiety and poor sleep patterns.

Passiflora
Calms the nervous system, relaxing muscles and releasing tension.

Valerian
Use a low dose during the day for remaining calm. Take a higher dose at night to aid sleep.

NETTLE RASH

Urtica (Stinging Nettle)
Effective for any red, itchy, bumpy rash.

NEURALGIA

Hypericum (St John's Wort)
Relieves nerve pain.

Petasites
Posesses antispasmodic properties and is excellent for pain relief.

NOSEBLEEDS — tendency

Vinca minor
Strengthens blood vessel tone.

OSTEOARTHRITIS

See ARTHRITIS

OTITIS MEDIA

See EARACHE

OVERWEIGHT

Helianthus tuberosis

Rebalances sugar levels and reduces cravings. Use with a calorie-controlled diet.

Kelp

Helps to balance metabolism, improving sluggish energy patterns and helping the body to detoxify.

PAIN RELIEF

Any of the following may help:

Petasites

Relieves muscle spasms.

Black Cohosh

Has pain-relieving properties. Do not use if suffering from breast cancer.

PERIOD PAIN

Agnus castus

Raises progesterone levels to rebalance hormone ratios. Take for at least three cycles to establish effect. If this is ineffective, try Black Cohosh.

Petasites

Possesses antispasmodic properties and is excellent for pain relief.

PMS (Premenstrual Syndrome)

Agnus castus

If symptoms include irritability, mood swings, breast tenderness and fluid retention.

Black Cohosh

If symptoms include depression, irregular periods and cramping pain. Do not use if suffering from breast cancer.

POST VIRAL FATIGUE SYNDROME

See CHRONIC FATIGUE SYNDROME

PRICKLY HEAT

Urtica (Stinging Nettle)

Removes uric acid from the body and lessens itching.

PROSTATE PROBLEMS

Saw Palmetto
Extremely effective at relieving symptoms.

PROSTATITIS

Saw Palmetto/Echinacea
In combination, they are anti-inflammatory and anti-infective for the prostate.

PSORIASIS

Aloe vera
Nourishing and cleansing.

Milk Thistle
Helps the liver detoxify the body.

Chamomile (German or Roman)
Anti-inflammatory and soothing for the skin.

Neem
Has anti-inflammatory properties. For external use only.

RAYNAUD'S DISEASE

See CIRCULATION

RHEUMATISM

See ARTHRITIS

RINGWORM

Echinacea/Spilanthes/Neem
All are antifungal.

SAD (Seasonal Affective Disorder)

Hypericum (St John's Wort)
Take throughout the winter to ward off SAD.

SCIATICA

Hypericum (St John's Wort)
Deals with nerve pain. Take the tincture internally and apply the oil externally.

SENILE DEMENTIA

Ginkgo biloba
For improving and maintaining memory.

SHINGLES

Petasites
Possesses antispasmodic properties and is excellent for pain relief.